ALASTAIR HUMPHREYS

TEN
LESSONS
FROM THE
ROAD

eye books

eyeOpener

Why is it that the wonderful childhood sense of grandeur and ambition that fills young imaginations is so often lost with the passage of time? When does it become acceptable to dismiss our wildest dreams and accept that the journey of life is pre-ordained? Take a moment to reflect on your accomplishments over the course of the past month. Now think about the past year, or the past ten years. If you discover an unsettling amount of predictability and monotony has crept into your life you are not alone. But take heart, "ordinary" people do extraordinary things.

Alastair Humphreys was able to break away from the predictable and ride his bicycle around the world. In *Ten Lessons from the Road*, Alastair shares what he learnt from his four-year journey to help those eager to pursue their dreams and confront the fears and doubts we all face in adversity.

At Eye Books we take pride in publishing tales of unique travels and incredible journeys. These stories focus not only on the physical, but also on the human elements of the undertaking. In his first two books, *Moods of Future Joys* and *Thunder and Sunshine*, Alastair challenges the way we see things. They don't just recount a great adventure as he cycles around the world, they articulate the trials and triumphs – both physically and mentally – he encountered within himself.

It is never too late to reclaim your dreams and accomplish what you really want out of life. Remember that any journey begins with a single step. In *Ten Lessons* Alastair challenges us to see things differently, breaking down seemingly distant dreams into achievable goals. And now you've made the first step by picking up this book, you're on your way.
Dan Hiscocks, Publisher Eye Books.

If you would like to learn more about the Eye Books community and the other books we publish, please visit our website at www.eye-books.com and join us in a wonderful world of adventure.

If you're not hurting, you're not riding hard enough.
If you're not hungry, you've eaten too much.
If you're not cold, you're carrying too many clothes.
If you know you will succeed, it's too easy.

Introduction

IF YOU'VE BEEN AROUND THE BLOCK A FEW TIMES AND LEARNT A LESSON OR TWO, THINK WHAT YOU MIGHT HAVE PICKED UP GOING ALL THE WAY ROUND THE WORLD. THAT'S WHAT I DID. I WENT ROUND THE WORLD. ON A BICYCLE.

I'm a depressingly ordinary guy who had an extraordinary dream. My dream was to cycle right the way round the world. My friends felt it was ridiculous: would not one continent be adventure enough? Few potential sponsors bothered even to send, 'Thanks, but No Thanks' replies. It took me four years of determined effort to prove the doubters wrong and achieve my dream: cycling back to the front door I had closed behind me 46,000 miles earlier.

But the biggest doubter of all was myself. When I began I never believed I was going to make it. I just wanted to see how much I was capable of. For the first two years of the expedition – at least – I didn't think I would succeed. It was, to paraphrase Mr. Dickens, the best of times and the worst of times.

But now, back home again after spending four years, mostly alone, hauling myself down the highways of five continents – at times exhausted, sick, lonely or afraid – I can look back with satisfaction at having persevered, and I can reflect on the lessons I learnt along the way. Lessons that will serve me well in my future life; in the office, at home, with my family, as well as out in the world's wild places. Lessons to help me try to pursue a happy, fulfilled, responsible life.

When hearing about my bike ride, people often say, "you must be so fit" or "I could never do what you did" or "I would never have the courage to do it." Rubbish. Total rubbish. I truly believe that anybody can cycle round the world. Sure, most people would not want to, but we all have our dreams, we all have potential, and we can all achieve more than we believe. The only hard thing is to have the guts to break the habits and dogmas that bind us, to just get on our bikes and begin riding.

I had plenty of time on the road to reflect on why I was doing my ride, what had motivated me to begin, what I was learning on the way, what was stopping me from stopping, as well as what I hoped to take from it all on into the future. I have broken down some of these lessons into ten simple chapters, illustrated with experiences from my journey and stunning photography that is sure to inspire and thrill. These are ten points that led to the accomplishment of the biggest venture of my life (so far), a success that in the beginning I felt was beyond me. I've included excerpts from my books *Moods of Future Joys* and *Thunder & Sunshine*.

Why only ten lessons? We all have just one life and the clock is ticking fast. We can't spend too long theorising about how we are going to live our lives – better that we get out and live them! So ten lessons should be enough for now. Let's get on and ride the roads we have always dreamed of riding – before it's too late.

Contents

Excerpts from *Moods of Future Joys* and *Thunder & Sunshine*
are indicated by my cycling silhouette.

You Want to do *What?*

WHAT DO YOU WANT TO ACHIEVE WITH YOUR LIFE? HOW DO YOU WANT TO LIVE YOUR LIFE? WHAT DO YOU WANT WRITTEN ON YOUR GRAVESTONE?

Nothing struck me as right. Nothing rang true. It all seemed like a compromise. The routes expected of me, the conventional procession towards a secure job, a sensible pension, a respectable-sized gravestone – the roads to 'success' – just did not appeal to me. It is easy to slip into roles that bear little resemblance to how we really wanted our lives to pan out.

Impossible is just a big word thrown around by small men who find it easier to live in the world they've been given than to explore the power they have to change it. Impossible is not a fact. It's an opinion. It's not a declaration. It's a dare. Impossible is potential. Impossible is temporary...

Impossible is nothing.

MUHAMMAD ALI

I did not want to be jolted with the realisation – years from now, while waiting one day in the rain for a bus – that life had passed me by. And so, tentatively at first, I began questioning things, asking myself what I really wanted.

I realised that if we want to buck the trend, to forge our own paths, and not to just do what is expected of us, we need to summon up the nerve to do what we really dream of doing – to think big – and to begin making the very most of our potential, our opportunities, our lives.

It was time to choose my road. I chose to leave everything that I was familiar with, everything that I knew and loved and enjoyed. I chose to leave my friends and family and girlfriend and country. I decided to let go of everything that makes a life normal, secure and conventionally happy. It is a selfish, ungrateful risk to give up all that makes you happy in the hope that you can find better. You risk not finding it. You risk finding it, and then never being satisfied again, yearning always for more. But I was looking for experiences that nothing – not the dimming light of old age nor financial ruin – could take away from me. It was uncertain travel that held an appeal, a luring magic, for me. The intoxicating release from conventional bonds, a chance for self-testing and self-discovery, and the rushing joy of being alive that I rarely felt at home. I chose to leave everything behind; the wasted opportunities, the shiny things I had spent money on, the ironing board and the expectations of conventional living, the race to get a bigger house, bigger car, bigger gravestone. I would have no home, no appointments, no deadlines, no career, no beautiful possessions, no weekend hobbies, no mortgage, no bills, no commute. I would have everything I wanted.

WHAT DO YOU WANT TO ACHIEVE WITH YOUR LIFE?
I want to make the most of my potential and my opportunities.

HOW DO YOU WANT TO LIVE YOUR LIFE?
Optimistically, ambitiously, generously and with good humour.

WHAT DO YOU WANT WRITTEN ON YOUR GRAVESTONE?
"He lived a good, full and worthwhile life."

DREAM EXTRAVAGANT DREAMS
At first I thought that I would like to cycle to India. I knew that that was possible; plenty of people had done it. But, looking at my atlas, it seemed a shame to stop at India. I would be halfway to Australia by then. I might as well keep going.

**Dreams make the impossible possible;
dedication makes the possible probable;
and work makes the probable happen.**

JIM TREFETHEN

accomplishments and wondered whether I could do anything remotely similar. There was only one way I would ever know.

DREAM BIG WITH HEART AND SOUL

I had my dream: to undertake an outrageous journey. I knew that I might well fail, but I also knew that aiming ridiculously high meant that I was likely to end up achieving more than if I had set a realistic and achievable target. There is something that *you* have always dreamed of doing. It's time to be bold, time to commit yourself to that dream.

PUSH AN IDEA TO THE LIMITS

Why not ride as far as it is possible to ride, to keep going until I arrived back where I began? Why not ride all the way around the planet? The idea seemed absurd. The idea became exciting.

LEGWORK AND PLANNING ARE NEEDED TO ACTIVATE A DREAM

But was it possible? How far was it? How long would it take? What should I take with me? The months before departure were exciting. I learnt so much. A lot of hard work went into getting ready to begin. I was inspired by life again. I absorbed book after book about great journeys and adventures and the men and women who had pulled them off. I marvelled at their

YOUR DREAM CAN BE ANYTHING YOU WANT. YOU JUST HAVE TO OWN IT, GUARD IT PRECIOUSLY AND TAKE THE NECESSARY STEPS TO LIVE IT FOR YOURSELF

What visionary dared to dream of building the Great Pyramids? Or conceived the idea of the Monastery at Petra?

BE REASSURED: SETTING YOURSELF, AND ACCOMPLISHING, OUTRAGEOUS GOALS BECOMES A HABIT

I was fortunate enough to attain my goal. Today, the realisation of that dream defines who I am, even when I attempt to move on to new things. It has shifted me to a different level than I was on before I began. People expect more of me now. I expect more of myself. More seems possible. The same will be true for you once you take the decision to kick-start your ambition.

YOURS IS THE WORLD

Imagine you are free. Totally free. Unfettered by commitments, finances, physique, intellect, talent, age, education and – critically – by your own perception of your capabilities. Imagine now that you have only 70 years of life on the most astonishing, improbable, wonderful planet that ever existed. The clock is ticking. The world is all before you. Go on, take whatever you want. Yours is the Earth, and everything that's in it. This is a supermarket sweep of infinite scope. It's all yours. What do you want? You are limited only by your imagination.

DREAM BIG

I am convinced that we consistently underestimate our capacities and our capabilities. We settle too low. We strive for what we know we can achieve. What's the point of that? Far better to be wildly ambitious, to set ourselves outrageous goals, and through that accomplish

far more than we dared believe possible. We should define our passions, define our goals, then set about achieving them.

Think of your many years of procrastination; how the gods have repeatedly granted you further periods of grace, of which you have taken no advantage. It is time now to realise that your time has a limit set to it. Use it, then, to advance your enlightenment; or it will be gone, and never in your power again.
MARCUS AURELIUS

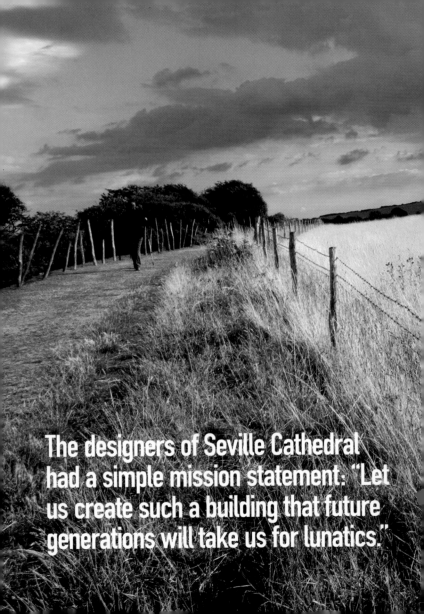

The designers of Seville Cathedral had a simple mission statement: "Let us create such a building that future generations will take us for lunatics."

Just do it

MAKE IT HARDER TO IGNORE YOUR DREAM THAN TO OVERCOME THE RISKS AND OBSTACLES INVOLVED. WHAT DIFFICULTIES DO YOU NEED TO OVERCOME IN ORDER TO BEGIN?

I often receive emails from people contemplating an expedition, a journey, or a change of lifestyle. They are looking for advice, for the comforting blanket of knowledge that, ironically, you can only acquire once you have begun, yet only seek beforehand. But most of all they are looking, consciously or sub-consciously, for one thing. They are looking for impetus.

Do, or do not. There is no try. YODA

My bags are packed and I can think of no convincing excuse to back out. I am trapped on a runaway train that I set in motion myself, but now am powerless to stop or jump off. I wake up feeling physically sick with fear. Excuses to delay race through my frightened mind. I roll out of my bed for the last time, open my curtains for the last time and look at my beautiful view of the Yorkshire Dales for the last time. I realise that if I take stock of all these 'last times', then I will be in floods of tears before I even make it downstairs (for the last time).

Everything seems surreal. Is this really happening to me? I don't have to do this, do I? I awkwardly wheel my heavy, cumbersome bike out of the garage, wait for Dad to ask the neighbour to take a final photo of the family, hug everyone goodbye and then I am off. As easy as that. I have crossed my first border: from being a person dreaming of his big journey to somebody who is actually on his journey.

Finally I round the corner and my home is gone. Then it all hits me. I have just left from my front door to try to cycle around the planet. I have left behind everyone that I love. I am alone. If I were a brave man, I would turn around right now, go home, and admit that it was too frightening. Instead I keep on riding.

Grab a pencil, grab a piece of paper. Draw a line down the middle. In one column make a list of all the reasons why you should begin taking steps to pursue your outrageous goal today. In the other column make a list of all the reasons not to bother and just to carry on with things the way they are. I'll help you out: 'Too expensive.' 'Can't get time off work.' 'Mortgage.' 'It's not "sensible".' 'I can't leave Bobby [my cat/my partner/my budgie].' 'It's not good for my career path.' 'It will affect my pension plan.' 'Too much effort.' 'I will miss episodes of "Big Brother"... Now, imagine you are 90 years old and on your last legs. (If you are already 90, well, congratulations! So imagine you're 100 instead.) Will you be pleased with these excuses to procrastinate and wriggle out of the biggest, most exciting chapter of your life when you're about to snuff it? Remember: he who dies with the most toys, still dies.

DO YOU BELIEVE YOUR EXCUSES?

Ignoring all the demons in my head, climbing on the bike, and pedalling away from my front door was the hardest thing I have done. It took all my resolve to ignore the excuses.

WHAT DIFFICULTIES DO YOU NEED TO OVERCOME IN ORDER TO BEGIN?

I was in a happy relationship, I had a good job waiting for me, I change and what awaited me if I persevered... I had to ensure that I did not lose sight of all that.

Let's then think of ways to overcome all the negativity and excuses of that second column and focus on all the positive reasons for why you will not regret beginning to do what you really want to do with your life.

Beginning is undeniably hard. What the people who get in touch with me really want is to be given courage

I was engulfed in so much doubt that it was difficult not to concede to those telling me I ought to limit my plans.

had all my friends and family in England. Convincing myself that there could be something even better waiting for me out there, and that I would regret it if I did not look for it, was very difficult.

The start of my ride round the world was tough to persevere through. I was engulfed in so much doubt that it was difficult not to concede to those telling me I ought to limit my plans. What I tried to always concentrate on during the difficult times was the memory of why I began the trip in the first place, how my life was before I began, how I had wanted it to

and reassurance, and for me to whisk away their carpet of complacency, to blast the starter's pistol, to put my boot squarely against their backs and shove them over the cliff edge that marks the point of no return. Reassurance, nerve and a boot in the back. I certainly had wished that there was somebody to do the same for me as my departure date loomed. Leaving behind a happy, comfortable life for one brim full of uncertainties and hardships was difficult. But I forced myself to begin, because I did not want to look back later in life and lament not having had a go at it.

Look, if you had one shot, one opportunity, to seize everything you ever wanted, would you capture it or just let it slip? EMINEM

> # Nothing will ever be attempted if all possible objections must first be overcome. SAMUEL JOHNSON

We need to overcome our inertia, to focus on the positives and all the possibilities that lie ahead. I needed only to get on my bike and ride. What small thing do you need to do in order to begin? Inertia, in life as in science, means that a body remains motionless until a force acts upon it. The larger the object, the more difficult it is to move it. So it is with life. The longer you have been stuck in your ways – doing the same things year in, year out, without questioning what you are doing, why you are doing it, and whether you wish to continue doing it – the harder it will be to get you moving. But, as you fight to overcome lethargy and doubt, lazy procrastination and fear, draw spirit from knowing that, in life as in science, once something builds up a good momentum it's hellish hard to stop it.

So, as you're struggling to get started (your devilish mind rolling out the excuses), be aware that beginning your journey is the hardest thing you'll ever do. However, if you can ignore them, ignore them and set off anyway, then you'll take some stopping!

YOU CAN'T IGNORE YOUR DREAM, CAN YOU?

Can you acknowledge, deep down, that you need to get on and do this thing? By all means look at the obstacles in your path, but look at them only with positive eyes that ask, "how am I going to get past this in order to get where I want to be?"

How we spend our days is, of course, how we spend our lives. ANNIE DILLARD

Until one is committed, there is hesitancy, the chance to draw back, always ineffectiveness. Concerning all acts of initiative (and creation), there is one elementary truth, the ignorance of which kills countless ideas and splendid plans: that the moment one definitely commits oneself, the providence moves too. A whole stream of events issues from the decision, raising in one's favor all manner of unforeseen incidents, meetings and material assistance, which no man could have dreamt would have come his way. W. H. MURRAY

Imagine you are old and looking back on your life.
Now – Just do it!

Quitting is Not an Option (But Failure is)

DOES A FEAR OF FAILING PREVENT YOU FROM BEGINNING THINGS? IF YOU QUIT, WHAT WILL YOU DO INSTEAD THAT IS MORE REWARDING?

Congratulations! You've overcome the pessimism and inertia. You're in motion. The hardest part is over. But getting out on the road and beginning the journey does not mean that the difficulties are over. Nothing worth doing is achieved lightly and there will be plenty of rough patches ahead. You need to begin to be able to balance a hunger for success with a sanguine, uninhibited approach to the possibility of failure.

Run if you can, walk if you have to, crawl if you must. But never, ever stop. Never stop. DEAN KARNAZES

In a windowless, filthy room in Damascus, I cried my eyes out: I was not going to make it round the world. I could not stick it out. I had bitten off more than I could chew. It was too hard. I was not up to it. I was going to fail. It was my dream life and I didn't want it anymore. I was absolutely on the brink of riding out to the airport to jack it all in and return home. I have never been so low in my life. It was the closest I ever came to surrendering.

"How did I have the audacity and arrogance to think that I could pedal through Africa?" I asked myself over and over, clutching for answers. "How could I have committed myself to years of this madness?"

I tried to focus on why I wanted to continue, hoping to highlight the positives. I had always said that if I ever found something better to do with my life than riding round the world, then I would do it: I did not begin the ride solely with the purpose of reaching the end. But I had not yet thought of (and still haven't) anything more exciting and rewarding to replace it. I knew that if I quit I was likely to regret it one day. I thought of how frustrated I had been with life in England, how eager to get away from comfortable complacency. I thought of all the experiences I would miss by going home. I was lucky. I had an ambition and I had the opportunity to pursue it. It was now or never for my dream of many years.

Was I going to give that up?

DOES A FEAR OF FAILING PREVENT YOU BEGINNING?

A fear of failing and a fear of what others would think about my failure certainly motivated me in the first couple of years on the road. I am grateful, however, that it did not prevent me from beginning in the first place. I felt that, with a project such as this, it was better to have a go than not to try at all.

IF YOU QUIT, WHAT WILL YOU DO INSTEAD THAT IS MORE REWARDING?

This was my mantra when times were tough. I never did think of anything better. And so I never quit. I also had a rule that I was not allowed to pack it all in when I was cold, tired, sick, hungry, or at night. I did not want to jump recklessly into doing something I would regret as soon as I cheered up. A memory bank of previous experiences – the cerebral version of an athlete's 'muscle memory' – helps you to see things through, confident in the knowledge that if you've done it before, surely you can do it again. Unfortunately this means that the first, most difficult step into the unknown is made even harder by having no memory bank of prior experiences to help stiffen your resolve.

A difficulty of setting bold goals is that for much of your journey you will travel alone, alone in your head, with no scaffolding of prior experience to prop you up, no memory of a previous path to guide you, no support from friends and family who have no experience with which to help you. Some will tell you that you are mad, and nearly all will say, 'what is the use?' Despair and doubt will be your all-too-frequent travel companions.

This is why quitting is not an option. The road you have chosen *will* be onerous and the serpent in your mind *will* twist and turn you towards the primrose-lined easy alternative. You'll come up with all sorts of excuses that justify giving the whole nonsense up. However, if you can persevere through it all, you will be stronger for the next time. You will have your rewards. You just have to get through the first time.

Whilst I am adamant about the rewards that are earned if you learn to detest quitting, I do not think you should worry about failure. If you take on difficult challenges, you will fail at many, if not most, of them. Fear of failure is something that strongly motivates us not to give up. But the dread of failure must not be so strong that we hesitate to even begin a task for fear of failing it. Dreading defeat is too often responsible for people not even beginning something. This stifles daring and stops you taking on the challenge that, if successful, could be the making of you. Sure, you may fail, but so long as you fought hard you should not look back on that with remorse. With a determination to improve, or act differently perhaps, but not with regret. But if you do not even have a go, there will be nothing to show later except bitter grumbles of "would've, could've, should've".

The excitement of hatching your dream is just a memory now. The injection of energy you received by taking the first steps on the long walk towards your outrageous goal has long since ebbed. You have taken a sobering reality check of how much hard graft lies ahead of you. You have begun to doubt your ability or

determination to see it through. You have even started to question whether it is even worth continuing. It is!

Step back through your memory to remember why you began this journey. Reflect on how excited you were to begin. You were excited because you knew well that the end result was important and alluring to you. Do not lose sight of that now.

Become comfortable in your mind that failing is not shameful; you must not let the fear of failure suffocate your desire to act. Remember how much you wanted this in the first place.

Now you will be free to act with bold determination, working towards something you desperately wish to accomplish.

Failing doesn't make you a failure.
Giving up, accepting your failure,
refusing to try again does! RICHARD EXELY

Dream big and dare to fail.

We Walk Alone

DO YOU BLAME OTHER PEOPLE FOR YOUR LIFE NOT BEING WHERE YOU WANT IT TO BE? OR ARE YOU WILLING TO TAKE THE RESPONSIBILITY AND OWNERSHIP FOR YOUR OUTRAGEOUS GOAL?

We all enjoy sitting back in a comfy armchair, pausing for a moment in complete contentment. These are times when we can look back on what we have done, and look forwards to all we would like to do. Times to think idealistically and set down the laws and standards by which we wish to live. To feel satisfied by

things done well and seen through to their ends. To feel disappointed by the occasions we listened to our own excuses and took a decision that was easy and appealing at the time, but which rings hollow now.

We can think forward to events that lie ahead and hope we will undertake them the right way, not the easy way. It is not easy to act with dignity and humility, to exercise grace under pressure. Far too often it is simpler to be lazy or selfish or complacent. It is comforting, if futile, to pin the blame on others. So it is important to assess coldly that many of our failures are down to ourselves, and to come to terms with the fact that, if we are going to succeed at something, then we have to take action ourselves.

Throughout my journey ran the constant thread of the self-imposed rules I set myself, the standards by which my quest had to stand up to my own harsh self-scrutiny. In some ways my whole journey was strangely contrived and artificial, yet its difficulty sometimes felt even larger by being arbitrary and self-chosen. There were no prizes, awards, trophies or records at stake. My route and journey would be as hard or as easy, as long or as short as I chose to make it. I was competing only with myself. I had to set myself problems and then solve them. It is hard to motivate yourself to build a high brick wall when you know that you have then to climb over it. It is a strange person too, who bangs his head ever harder against that brick wall because he knows that the harder he bangs, the sweeter the stopping will feel.

The ride was important to me, to my future, to my self-confidence, to all the hard work I had gone through to get to this point. And yet, I was always wryly aware that it was only a bike ride. It didn't really *matter*.

DO YOU BLAME OTHER PEOPLE FOR YOUR LIFE NOT BEING WHERE YOU WANT IT TO BE?

This is such an easy trap to fall into, and I am too often guilty of it. When I was planning my expedition a large part of me wanted to find somebody to join me on the road. However, a smaller part of me argued that I really should make the journey alone. That way things were far clearer; if I succeeded, it was because of myself. If I failed, then I could have no excuses save those explanations that centred on me. I would fall, or I would walk, by myself.

ARE YOU WILLING TO TAKE THE RESPONSIBILITY FOR YOUR OUTRAGEOUS GOAL?

I dreamt up my outrageous goal. There were very few people who had experience that could help me. From an early stage in my preparations, it was clear that no companies were going to sponsor me. I was on my own. Perhaps all this helped me take responsibility for my project. If I did not take steps to make something happen, it did not happen.

There is a powerful prayer, resonant for anyone unable to be satisfied with comfortable satisfaction. The prayer asks God for "What one cannot demand from oneself... I don't ask You for rest, or quiet, whether of soul or body... I don't ask for wealth, nor for success, nor even health perhaps. That sort of thing You get asked for so much that You can't have any of it left. Give me, Lord, what you have left over. Give me what no-one wants from You. I want insecurity, strife, and I want You to give me these once and for all so that I can be sure of having them always, since I shall not always have the courage to ask You for them."

It reminds me not to settle for the easy option.

Don't ask yourself what the world needs. Ask yourself what makes you come alive, and go do that, because what the world needs is people who have come alive. JOHN ELDRIDGE

Bugle calls to quit a job you hate are not always realistic. Drum-beating shouts to do this and that are not for everybody. A more subtle change of tack may be more appropriate. Soften it, mould it to your own circumstances. But hold this one thing clear, whatever your situation: this is your life and you have the right to live it well. With rights come responsibilities, but you cannot do full justice to your commitments; to your family, your business, bank manager or parole officer, if you are not content. If you feel that you are not able, or not bold enough, to take giant leaps, take a small step. If you feel anxious about the consequences of changing the equilibrium, if you feel lost or beyond changing, take a tiny step and test the waters. We walk with small steps at first.

In 1995 Poppa Neutrino sailed a homemade raft from North America to Europe, becoming the second person to sail a raft across the Atlantic Ocean, and the first to do so on a junk raft. Nobody thought that it could be done. But he believed in himself, and he succeeded.

Set yourself a tiny goal, but make sure that you achieve it. Read a book instead of watching reality TV tonight. Eat an apple instead of a chocolate bar. Walk up the steps when you get off the Tube instead of taking the escalator. Realise that you accomplished it all alone, assess if it makes you feel a little better, then set yourself another small task. The days will pass and your confidence will grow and your ambition will increase. You will do more with your days and your horizons will spread wider. Nobody else will care if you take the easy option or not. It's up to you.

A Bad Day is a Good Day

BAD TIMES WILL COME. WHAT CAN YOU DRAW STRENGTH FROM WHEN THINGS BECOME DIFFICULT? HOW ARE YOU GOING TO DEAL WITH THE HARD PATCHES?

The pursuit of your outrageous goal will not always run smoothly. As well as the doubt and the fatigue within you, you will come up against obstacles and hindrances. You *will* have bad days. We need to condition our minds and spirits to feel that the bad days are inevitable, that they will pass, and that they make the end result all the sweeter. In Siberia I was joined by a good friend, and we rode like madmen through the brutal awfulness of winter in a crazy race against time to get out of Russia before our visas expired. Those three months have blended in my mind into a single, blurred memory of fatigue, stress, and appalling cold.

It doesn't have to be fun to be fun. MARK TWIGHT

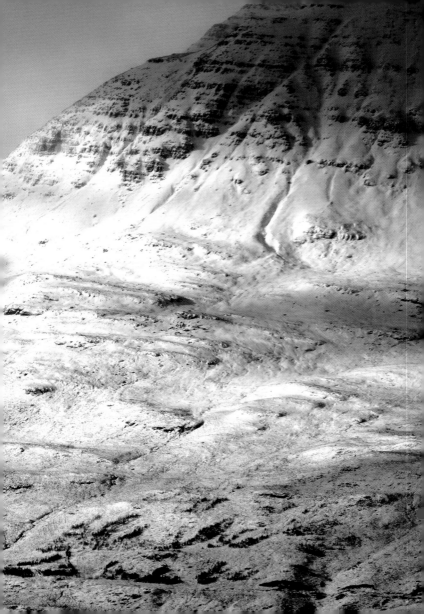

Siberia is a beautiful, pure but daunting land. We skidded and slid and fell and bruised. Some days the skies were grey and pregnant with more snow, others were bright like a new razor-shining, slicing.

It was -40°C and the elastic in our tent poles was no longer elasticised. It took about an hour to fix this and my fingers suffered even in gloves as I worked to tie and untie fiddly knots and thread elastic through the narrow tent poles. Bare fingers stuck to metal. It was horrible to be painfully cold when you knew that there were no more clothes to wear, no possibility of calling it a day and heading somewhere warm and nothing to do but endure.

We were riding as hard as we could, but the roads were covered in ice and snow. Progress was slow. Our bikes were massively heavy. We were hampered by our bulky clothes. We often had to run or walk with the bikes to get some feeling back into our numb toes. We had so far to ride that I refused to allow myself to call an end to a day's ride, pushing it on until we were exhausted and frozen and could no longer hold our eyes open. Through those grisly night rides, riding blind through the slippery darkness, I longed, mile after mile, for Rob to quit, to say that he had had enough for the day, just so that I could agree and we could escape into the dubious sanctuary of the tent. Spending 15 hours on the road, skidding and crashing throughout, and then pitching camp in deep snowdrifts and thawing ice to cook, left us barely five hours of sleep each night until the next day began in the pitch darkness of 5 am. We still had 2,000 miles of Siberia to get through, but we were not stopping.

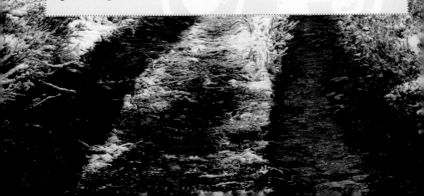

WHAT CAN YOU DRAW STRENGTH FROM WHEN THINGS BECOME DIFFICULT?

When times were tough I used to think about my friends, my family and all the people who had helped get me where I was in my life. I imagined them lining the road, cheering me on like the crowds at a marathon. I knew that they all wanted me to succeed and so I didn't want to let them down.

BAD TIMES WILL COME. HOW ARE YOU GOING TO DEAL WITH THEM?

A sense of humour was invaluable in trying to keep things in perspective. My struggles and bad days were utterly trivial in comparison to many people's and I tried hard to keep things in perspective. This was sometimes easier said than done!

Before travelling to Siberia I pondered for a long time about where best to 'begin' the Asian portion of my ride. Singapore appealed, Shanghai too.

Anywhere along the eastern shore of the continent would have been acceptable. But I had been riding for so long now that I felt that I could not let my standards slip. So I tried to imagine myself as an old man, looking back on

my life. What memories would I like to have? The answer was clear. I should take the most difficult, original option possible.

And so I found myself in Siberia. It was cold, miserable, daunting, stressful, awful. But now, warm and home once more, I appreciate those days almost above all others on my ride.

REMEMBER HOW MUCH YOU WANTED TO BEGIN.

When things get tough and you question the worth of carrying on, cast your mind back to how you felt when you began. Remember the enthusiasm you felt, and how desperate you were to succeed. Recall why you started, and look forward to how worthwhile it will be if you can grit through this difficult period.

IF IT WERE EASY, EVERYBODY WOULD BE DOING IT.

If your goal is suitably outrageous and challenging there will be few others who share your passion and determination, so you will walk mostly alone. At times this will be tough. But that surely is a reason to continue, not to quit.

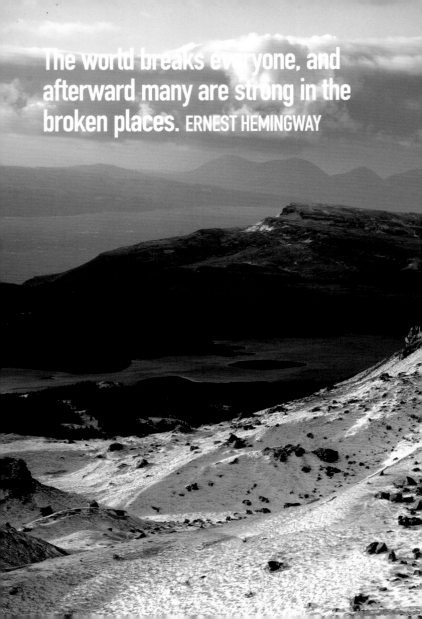
The world breaks everyone, and afterward many are strong in the broken places. ERNEST HEMINGWAY

IT DOESN'T HAVE TO BE FUN TO BE FUN.

Develop a sense of the absurd. Learn to laugh at the ridiculousness of your situation, and at yourself. Don't take things too seriously. Remember that there are sensations other than pleasure that are good to experience: determination, grace under pressure, and a zen-like calm when all about you are losing their heads!

deprived of sleep, riding hard for crazy hours and freezing cold as well. I hated it. I was exhausted. I wanted to go home.

But I tried to end each day positively. As I lay shivering in my sleeping bag I would try to learn from my mistakes. And I had not given up, I had made it through the day: that gave me strength to face tomorrow.

Every night I asked myself what the best part of the day

Those days in Siberia were the hardest physical days of my life so far...

T. E. Lawrence (of Arabia) had written 250,000 words of his autobiography when he lost the manuscript whilst changing trains at Reading Station. Despite national newspaper appeals to find the "hero's manuscript", it was never found. Working from memory alone he sat down and wrote 400,000 words in the next three months. Today his *Seven Pillars of Wisdom* remains an epic of 20th Century literature.

Those days in Siberia were the hardest physical days of my life so far. For three months we were

had been. Maybe it had only been a hot cup of tea. But there is always something good. And I would ask myself what I was looking forward to tomorrow. It may only be another cup of tea, or simply the end of the next day's riding, but there was always something positive ahead. To shiver in a frost-rimed tent is to truly appreciate the next warm duvet. A parched desert teaches deep gratitude for running water. Clarion calls to be alive and to treasure life. On the road you learn to appreciate

a simplification of life. When we made it out of Russia – with a single day to spare on our visas – I felt intensely satisfied. To have stuck through the bad times taught me so much about both my strengths and my weaknesses.

I felt proud to have made it and determined to capitalise on the lessons learnt in the worst days.

Ye who have suffered great trials gather courage, perhaps one day it will be pleasant to remember them...

Leaders must be tough enough to fight, tender enough to cry, human enough to make mistakes, humble enough to admit them, strong enough to absorb the pain, and resilient enough to bounce back and keep on moving. JESSE JACKSON

Be Brutally Honest with yourself

HOW COMMON IT IS TO HEAR EXCUSES. TALES OF BAD LUCK, INJUSTICE, FOILED PLANS, ALL THE FAULT OF SOMEBODY ELSE. IT IS HARD TO ACCEPT THAT YOU HAVE DONE BADLY OR MADE MISTAKES.

I am always happy to absolve myself of responsibility and blame somebody else. But I am learning, slowly, that in order to remain clear-sighted about what I am trying to achieve, it is helpful to be honest and self-aware. I am learning not to believe my own excuses.

There are two types of people in this world; people who find excuses, and people who find ways through, round, and over their obstacles. ALASTAIR HUMPHREYS

If you were to die right now, how would you feel about your life? FIGHT CLUB

My journey round the world was, most of the time, a solo activity. My success or failure did not particularly impact on anybody else. Alone, I became extremely self-aware, very conscious of my moods and my subconscious feelings. I knew my physical capacity and my mental strengths and weaknesses.

I knew that my body could hold out longer than my mind could. And so my expedition became one fought out, more and more, within my own head. Curiously, the fate of my ride around the world was likely to be determined by the journeys inside my mind.

I was only too eager to blame things on anything but my own shortcomings. However, the long, slow, quiet miles allowed much time for introspection. Time to whittle away the excuses and to allow the open sores to heal. Time to acknowledge my limitations and to feel stronger for having done that. Paradoxically, perhaps, if you are willing to admit your weaknesses to yourself, then they stop being weaknesses.

What Do You Really Want?

IS THIS YEAR IMPORTANT TO YOU? WHEN DID YOU LAST THINK, "WHAT DO I REALLY WANT?"

Is this year important to you? Then use it! Make a New Year's resolution today. The peak age for running a marathon, something that many people consider vaguely as being on their 'Things to Do in Life' list (and if it isn't on your list, it should be!), is generally acknowledged to be between 30 and 40 years of age.

If you are aged 20 now, and procrastinating signing up for a marathon, then each year that you waste is at least 5% of your potential. If you are 30 now, each escaped year is some 10% of your best opportunities gone. Imagine voluntarily agreeing to give up 10% of your lifespan! If you are over 40 now, do not despair. You may not be able to achieve the best marathon time that you could have run years ago, but you can still run a marathon. And the older you are the greater that achievement will be.

IS THIS YEAR IMPORTANT TO YOU?

I worry at times that each year is almost too important to me. I dislike birthdays for their celebration of another year gone. I feel a tremendous pressure to make the most of each year, to make all my days as full and worthwhile as possible.

WHEN DID YOU LAST THINK, "WHAT DO I REALLY WANT?"

Returning home from four years on the road, it took me a long time to decide what to do next with my life, how to make the

"The years thunder by, the dreams of youth grow dim where they lie caked in dust on the shelves of patience. Before we know it, the tomb is sealed." So I chose to leave everything that I was familiar with, everything that I knew and loved and enjoyed. I turned down a good job offer. I chose to leave my friends, family, girlfriend and country. I decided to let go of everything that makes a life normal, secure and conventionally happy. Like the movie poster blu-tacked to the wall in my student halls, I chose not to "choose a big television, choose fixed-interest mortgage repayments, choose a starter home, choose sitting on the couch watching mind-numbing, spirit-crushing game shows." I chose something else. I was tremendously excited by life and I didn't think that I would find it where I was. I knew that leaving would be hard, but, like Candide, "I should like to know which is worse, to be raped a hundred times by negro pirates, to have a buttock cut off, to run the gauntlet among the Bulgarians, to be whipped and flogged in an auto-da-fé, to be dissected, to row in a galley, in short to endure all the miseries through which we have passed, or to remain here doing nothing?"

My mother-in-law and I ran the London Marathon the same year. When I crossed the finish line she was just reaching the halfway point. Whose achievement was the greater? Mine for running it quickly, or hers for completing an event twice as long as mine? My mother-in-law certainly gained more from the experience and, rightly so, has a greater sense of achievement than I do. Only those who have run a marathon can call themselves marathon runners.

next year as rewarding as the last. So I spent a lot of time thinking about my life and what I wanted from it.

Perhaps you have more sense than to want to run a marathon. No problem. But we all have our own 'marathon'. A watershed

moment in life. Something that you will use as a marker. My life before 'x' and my life after 'x'. Something we would love to accomplish, something difficult (that, at times, will seem to be *too* difficult). Remember, failing is acceptable. It is looking back with regrets that is not. The time to act is now. Sign up now for a marathon, a half marathon, a 10k, a fun run. You'll never put your trainers on and get fit if you don't. Join a Spanish class. Learn how to use your camera properly. Quit your job and do something you love. Do something you care about. Do something to add value to the planet. Every year is a significant percentage of all your time that remains on this spectacular place we call Earth and home. The older you become the greater that percentage is. The younger you are the more lasting your change can be.

So, whatever your age, whatever your personal marathon: Act Now. Put down this book and take one step towards making the most of this year.

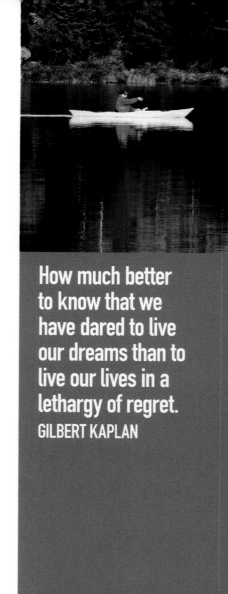

How much better to know that we have dared to live our dreams than to live our lives in a lethargy of regret.
GILBERT KAPLAN

Life is not lost by dying; life is lost minute by minute, day by dragging day, in all the thousand small uncaring ways. STEPHEN BENET

Think Like a Goldfish

Does your outrageous goal seem like a tiny dot on a distant horizon? Worse still, perhaps it is not even in sight – hidden far beyond the horizon, over hostile mountains and unimaginable rivers. This is not a time to be discouraged. Nor is it a time for thoughtful reflection and introspection. It is time to disengage your brain. If goldfish do indeed have but a 3-second memory, they would have no difficulties here. All we need to do in order to reach our far-off goal is just to keep moving. Certainly it may take a long time, and the way will be arduous. But if we can ignore all that, it is actually very simple to take just one small step.

Nothing is particularly hard if you divide it into small jobs. HENRY FORD

The morning I began riding from Patagonia to Alaska, I found it even harder than usual to get out of my sleeping bag. How do you persuade yourself to leave a nice warm sleeping bag and begin cycling, when 17,848 kilometres lie between you and your destination? From Ushuaia, the world's southernmost city, to Prudhoe Bay, on the shore of the Arctic Ocean in northern Alaska. Staying in bed seemed a far more attractive option. All the riding I had done counted for nothing now. I was back at the beginning, a brand new start at the bottom of a continental landmass, whose top was one third of the circumference of the globe away. I was intimidated by the road ahead. The old self-doubt rose through me. But I was going to enjoy this ride up the Americas. I was determined. I climbed onto my bike and began to pedal, away from one sea towards another distant one. Come on, Al, let's go have some fun! Just ride your bike for a day. That's all you need to think about. A fun day ride. An easy day ride. String those day rides together, but don't think about any more than each single, precious day. I took the first pedal strokes of millions, turning up the crunching dirt track through the lichen-covered forest, away from the sea, back into Ushuaia and out the other side. It was mid-February. I hoped to reach Alaska by the end of summer next year. My ride up the Americas was underway.

When I arrived in Prudhoe Bay, on the northern coast of Alaska, eighteen months after leaving Patagonia, the southernmost part of South America, I was amazed to have made it. Reflecting back I thought about my map. All the red lines of roads and yellow blobs of towns had been transformed in my mind. They were now real memories for me, fleshed out and brought to life by hundreds and hundreds of day trips. If you ride enough day trips, you can make it round the world.

WHAT NEXT TINY STEP DO YOU NEED TO TAKE TO EDGE YOU TOWARDS YOUR GOAL?
I am currently working towards an expedition in Antarctica, skiing all the way to the South Pole. Logistically it is a larger project than anything I have

done before. The budget, the equipment, the strategy: there is so much to do. But first, all my current steps are directed towards finding sponsors.

Things were looking good. I had set my goal. I had taken steps to begin it. I had not quit when times were hard, and I was still going. I had got through some bad times and had many more good times. But that did not mean I had the job nailed. I still had so, so far to go. And when I thought about the end it seemed so far away, so unattainable, that I would sometimes grow really discouraged.

Although we need to think big and bold in coming up with our goals, and have the tenacity to back ourselves to begin them, it's not a good idea to think too often about the far-off destination. I found the journey to be far more manageable if I adopted the memory span of a goldfish, thinking only about the next minute step I needed to take to keep on moving in the direction of my ultimate destination. If we only think as far ahead as the next faltering step, every journey is manageable.

Kaizen is a Japanese philosophy that focuses on continuous improvement throughout all aspects of life. The entire workforce is encouraged to continually think of new, small improvements that can be made. Little by little this leads to great success.

You are capable of so much more than you imagine. You have within your grasp virtually whatever target you set your sights on. To get there may not be easy. It may take your whole life, but if you are sufficiently determined, patient, bold and imaginative, you can reach it. If you think only in small increments, you need not grow disheartened. Act only on the next tiny step ahead of you. And if even that appears too large, then figure out how to break it down smaller still. Walk on through the rain, though your dreams be tossed and blown. Walk on, walk on with hope in your heart and you will arrive someday.

Though the way is full of perils, and the goal far out of sight, there is no road to which there is no end: do not despair. HAFEZ

Whatever you can do or dream you can, begin it. Boldness has genius, power and magic in it!
GOETHE

Shed a Load. Hit the Road

SAVE THE EARTH, SAVE YOURSELF. ARE YOU FIT ENOUGH? IF NOT, WHY DON'T YOU DO SOMETHING ABOUT IT?

I am no bronzed and muscled gym god. I suspect that you are not one either. That is not what this chapter is about. It is about being healthy, increasing your self-respect and enabling you to perform better in every aspect of your life.

Lack of activity destroys the good condition of every human being, while movement and methodical physical exercise save it and preserve it. PLATO

I am no athletic superstar. I was never in any sports teams at school. I realised sadly young that I was never going to play for Leeds United. In Los Angeles I nearly lost an arm wrestle to a 50-year-old woman.But by the end of my journey I was riding for more hours a day than cyclists do during the Tour de France. I could eat as much food as I wanted to, and I would not get fat, and I could sing at the top of my lungs as I rode smoothly and efficiently up Alpine mountain passes. I felt tired but satisfied at the day's end. It felt good.

I am not advocating an obsessive fitness regime, nor any fitness regime at all, actually. Rather I encourage people to remember the benefits a healthy lifestyle can bring.

ARE YOU FIT ENOUGH?

I am lucky. I am healthy, I'm not sick or injured. I live in a country with hospitals and clean water. Things are on my side. But I also do what I can to keep things that way. I eat pretty healthily. I like eating, and I eat a lot, but I don't eat vastly more calories than I use. When it's raining and cold and I really don't want to go out for a run, I understand that it's good for me so I just do it anyway.

WHY DON'T YOU DO SOMETHING ABOUT IT?

It's not easy to drag myself out of bed at 6am to run or swim or go to the gym before work. Every so often my weak side wins and I just roll over and go back to sleep, but usually I manage to beat the sleep demons, get out of bed, splash cold water on my face, and head out to do some

The ride had been a powerful learning experience for me. I had much to reflect on. I hoped not to lapse back into the sedentary life of our rich world, where even children do virtually no exercise and are prevented from taking risks. We drive everywhere, we eat crap food, we slouch indoors and we forget that doing exercise is something that makes you feel good, not bad. We eat too much, we run too little. Healthy mind and healthy body: how mad we are to neglect our body, the very machine that carries all our thoughts, emotions, ambitions, dreams, fears and even our life itself. And yet we still expect to live smoothly, healthily and happily to a ripe old age.

I had overestimated the physical side of the expedition. My body had gradually strengthened and hardened to meet the challenges of the road. It was a real thrill to have become so fit. To ride 100 miles a day, spending eight hours in the saddle on a laden bike over demanding terrain and to be able to wake the next morning and do it all again, and again, and again was something I was very grateful for. We greatly underestimate our bodies. People I met used to say to me, "I could never ride that far." For most people that was nonsense. I am no sporting superstar. I just do it!

exercise. And I never, ever regret it once I've done it. Never.

Far less than half the adult population of Britain does what the government recommends to be the minimum level of physical activity required for good health (and they include walking to the shops in their criteria!). If that applies to you, do yourself a favour. Even if you don't want to play a sport, have no desire to run a marathon, and do not feel the need to test your physical limits until you throw up, just do something for your health's sake. Go for an occasional walk, and promise yourself that you will stick at it for a couple of months.

Alex Vero was a 16-stone obese documentary filmmaker. He decided to turn his life around and see how far his fitness could progress in a two-year period – with the ultimate goal of attempting to qualify for the Beijing Olympic Games! He didn't quite make the Games, but he did manage to make TIME magazine and revitalize his life.

Push through the pain and the stiffness and the embarrassment and the reluctance and, after a while, you'll begin to feel better for exercising. You'll start to lose those wobbly bits, both physical and mental. You'll have more energy, more enthusiasm for life. Keep going a bit longer and you'll miss exercise when you don't do it. It's not always easy. When rain and wind rattled my tent in some soggy, grey dawn the last thing I wanted to do was get up and ride my bike for eight hours. Back home, I sometimes regret days when I couldn't be bothered to go for a run. But I never regret it once I've been.

Being fit feels good.

Those who do not find time for exercise will have to find time for illness. EARL OF DERBY

10

The World is a Good Place

THIS FINAL CHAPTER IS NOT REALLY A CALL-TO-ARMS, NOR IS IT PARTICULARLY ENCOURAGING YOU TO CHANGE ANYTHING IN YOUR LIFE.

I just wanted to end the book positively, and what more positive thing could I do than to try to remind you what a good and wonderful world we live in.

When I left home to try to cycle round the world I was worried about many different things. Friends, family and people I met along the way worried about only one thing on my behalf: my safety.

The world is a dangerous and wicked place. We all know that: we watch the news. Wars, murder, knife crime, terrorists.... This daily diet floods into our lives. We become bigoted and paranoid. We become afraid. The world is a bad place.

Yet if one good thing, and one thing alone, came out of my journey round the world, it was the realisation (or perhaps the reminding) that the world is essentially a *good* place and a suitable place for us to live out meaningful, rewarding and fulfilling lives.

Generosity, openness and trust were evident wherever I travelled. Perhaps I was exposed to these traits more often than in a normal life because of how I was travelling. I was always a novelty, I was young and broke and

wandering free. I was potentially vulnerable, but I forced myself to be open and trusting and to smile a lot and it was reciprocated in waves. Strangers inviting me to stay and rest in their homes. Cars stopping to hand me an orange or a bottle of water. Villages in Africa permitting me to stay in the chief's hut. People phoning radio stations to offer me their own bikes to replace my dying one. Schoolchildren baking me a birthday cake. A family lending me their home for a week while they were on holiday. The Yakut people in Russia whisking me

Camping one night beside a large haystack in a village, high in the highlands of Peru, I chatted for a couple of hours with a gathering of villagers. They sat around and shared their evening relaxation time with me. I began to set up my stove to prepare my dinner. But the people motioned me to stop. It had already been taken care of. Minutes later a young woman walked carefully down the field from the houses, carrying a tray with a bowl of soup and a plate of chicken and rice for my dinner. The woman watched me eat until my plate was empty and she was satisfied that the gringo had enjoyed her cooking. People who invited me into their homes often worried that I would not be able to eat 'their' kind of food. But an enjoyment and appreciation of food brought us closer together; it was something we could share and enjoy together whatever linguistic and cultural barriers stood between us. The villagers appreciated the concept of my journey, of adventure and wanderlust and seeing the world while I was young. They offered their support, asking what they could do to help. I told them that they were already helping me so much, as evenings like those made it all worthwhile. To feel at ease and welcome when you are far from home is one of the sweetest feelings of travelling.

in out of the cold. Cars on five continents beeping their support and encouragement. Thousands of people allowing me to fill my water bottles at their home or shop or village well. All the people who smiled and shared a joke and made me feel that I was not far from home, but actually at home in the world. Don't believe what you see on the TV: the world really is a good place. A good place to set outrageous goals, to achieve them, and to make the very most out of life.

AND FINALLY:
SIMPLIFY YOUR LIFE
Slash away all that is superfluous. Get rid of everything – material possessions, emotional ties, time commitments, resentments – everything that does not add happiness to your life or the lives of others.

Walk away from all that constrains and constricts you. Simplify your life and you will benefit.

Fear less, hope more; whine less, breathe more; talk less, say more; hate less, love more, and all good things are yours.

SWEDISH PROVERB